TIPS AND
TOOLS

A Guide to Effective Case Writing

TIPS AND TOOLS

A Guide to Effective Case Writing

Havovi Joshi

Singapore Management University, Singapore

 **World Scientific**

NEW JERSEY · LONDON · SINGAPORE · BEIJING · SHANGHAI · HONG KONG · TAIPEI · CHENNAI · TOKYO

Published by

World Scientific Publishing Co. Pte. Ltd.
5 Toh Tuck Link, Singapore 596224
USA office: 27 Warren Street, Suite 401-402, Hackensack, NJ 07601
UK office: 57 Shelton Street, Covent Garden, London WC2H 9HE

British Library Cataloguing-in-Publication Data
A catalogue record for this book is available from the British Library.

TIPS AND TOOLS
A Guide to Effective Case Writing

ISBN 978-981-3278-43-1

For any available supplementary material, please visit
https://www.worldscientific.com/worldscibooks/10.1142/11215#t=suppl

Desk Editor: Sandhya Venkatesh

Typeset by Stallion Press
Email: enquiries@stallionpress.com

Printed in Singapore

CONTENTS

ACKNOWLEDGEMENTS

There are many people who have helped me along the way as I wrote this book, and perhaps no one more than Philip Zerrillo, PhD. Thank you Dr Z, for all your encouragement and support, and being the most wonderful mentor!

I also want to extend a very special thanks to my husband, Rohit, for his constant love and support. This book is for you, Rohit.

To my parents, Shireen and Bomi Heerjee, I cannot thank you enough for your love and guidance, and teaching me that there is no end to learning. Thank you also to Pushpa and Ravindra Kumar Joshi, for their support and encouragement at every turn. To my siblings — Trista and Cyrus, Kaizad and Shernaz — a big thank you for always being there for me!

This book on case writing was first conceived some six years back, when Dr Z had just put together a small team to start off the case writing journey at SMU. So my next set of thanks is to two of the finest writers I have had the privilege to work with — Anne-Valerie Ohlsson and Kevin Sproule — what fun those days were!

In fact, I owe my gratitude today to each and every member of this case writing team. To Sarita Mathur, a dear friend and colleague, thanks for editing the first draft of this book in your inimitable style — gentle and yet, ever so thorough. Adina Wong, thank you for seeing all our projects through to completion and for always being there to help me out. Irene Soh, we would struggle to function without you! Lipika Bhattacharya, Sheetal Mittal, Alvin Lee, Sheila Wan, Chi Wei Chan, Christopher Dula, Cheah Sin Mei and Suh Wen Tan — the effort you all put in to produce quality output truly inspires me. Most of all, thanks to each one of you for being a super-fun bunch of colleagues that make work such a happy place!

I would also like to thank a number of the faculty at SMU who have taught me a great deal about writing high-quality cases and teaching notes. Srinivas Reddy, Arnoud de Meyer, Raj Srivastava, Roy Chua, Nirmalya Kumar, Kapil Tuli, Howard Thomas, Jochen Reb, Saumya Sindhwani and Tan Swee Liang — a very big thank you to each one of you for the unstinting support and guidance.

There are three other people I must extend my gratitude to. Jeroen van den Berg, Assistant Director, Asia Case Research Centre at The University of Hong Kong — over a decade back, you were the person who believed that I could write a case study, and invested so much of your time and energy in developing this novice writer! Thank you very much. Likewise, a special thanks to Indranil Bose, professor of MIS and Co-ordinator of the IIM-Calcutta Case Research Center, who was the faculty assigned to the first ever case I wrote — and did not give up on me despite that first draft! Thank you also to Professor Ali Farhoomand, the founding Director of the Asia Case Research Centre at The University of Hong Kong, for all his valuable comments and insights.

A very special thanks to Ophelia, Radhika, Kavita, Niloufer, Vandana, Urvashi, Shibani, Haritha, Kalpana and Anju for being such wonderful friends.

Amit and Gauri, you both inspire me every day.

And finally, to my children, Rhea and Rohan, I am so lucky to have you both. Thank you for making my life such fun at every turn!

Thank you all.

PREFACE

There has been a surge of interest in writing Asian-based case studies for the classroom over the past decade. This is particularly noticeable in schools located in Asia that understand the case methodology and recognise the value of teaching with cases, specifically cases that are written in a uniquely Asian context.

It is not surprising that an overwhelming proportion of cases presently available are about Western firms operating in the developed markets. After all, for several decades (in fact from 1910 or so onwards when Harvard Business School began to formally use cases in the classroom), cases were primarily confined to the large business schools in the US and Canada that invested heavily in this pedagogy. However, today we see a number of Asian schools and organisations that are actively engaged in writing and teaching with cases — with a focus on providing the Asian context.

It was with this objective, of filling a critical need for developing business case studies based on an Asian context for use in international curriculums, that Singapore Management University (SMU) established the Case Writing Initiative (CWI) in August 2011. The CWI team has since written over 200 cases, several of which have won awards in prestigious international case competitions. Additionally, CWI has conducted over 50 case writing and case teaching workshops in the region for faculty as well as practitioners in corporate firms and public sector organisations.

This book is based in a large part on the learnings that we have had from these workshops, as well as our own experience in developing cases at the university, working alongside some of the finest faculty at SMU. It offers a simple roadmap to guide those interested in writing their own case studies, and is full of very practical tips and insights.

Chapter 1

INTRODUCTION

Recognising the role of case studies in preparing students for their careers by developing a range of skills, as also varying the learning environment in the classroom, there is a high and growing support for case methodology across the world. This book is focused on providing a set of very practical tips and tools for novice case writers to commence on their case writing journey, and for experienced writers to further hone their skills.

What is a Case Study?

Before proceeding any further, it would help to remove any confusion on what a case study signifies in the context of this book. Oftentimes, a case study can be mistaken for a business case, which in fact is a business plan. Or it is misunderstood to be a research case study, which is typically a description of a business, or a legal issue, or a medical situation, that may include the writer's analysis and solution to the issues raised. For the purpose of this book, a case study refers to cases that are being written and used as a pedagogical tool for classroom discussion.

Gary Thomas offers the following definition of a case study:

Case studies are analyses of persons, events, decisions, periods, projects, policies, institutions, or other systems that are studied holistically by one or more methods. The case that is the subject of the inquiry will be an instance of a class of phenomena that provides an analytical frame — an object — within which the study is conducted and which the case illuminates and explicates.[1]

The Case Centre, the largest repository of business cases, states,

Case studies recount real life business or management situations that present participants with a dilemma or uncertain outcome. The case describes the scenario in the context of the events, people and factors that influence it and enables students to identify closely with those involved.[2]

To put it more simply, cases describe real-life situations, and typically put the participants in the shoes of the key decision maker, referred to as the protagonist, pushing them to discuss options for a dilemma faced by this protagonist, and propose possible solutions to the issue, having understood the benefits and problems of such an approach. It is to be noted that the case is not a piece of research, as it may deliberately falsify data to enhance the teaching value, or in some cases to disguise the company or protagonist. And one should not quote them for factual support or accuracy.

The initiative for writing a case typically originates either with a faculty and or an organisation. Faculty generally engage in the case writing process to develop a pedagogical instrument with specific learning objectives in mind. It is the need to teach particular concepts or principles that drives their case journey. As they seek to build the best teaching tool, the faculty may test the case in the classroom, and through the ensuing discussions, case studies are often further refined before publication.

---

[1] Gary Thomas. (2011). A typology for the case study in social science following a review of definition, discourse, and structure. *Qualitative Inquiry*, 17(6), 511–521.
[2] ECCH, as sourced from McNergney RF and McNergney, JM (2008). Education: The Practice and Profession of Teaching Pearson.

Organisations may also initiate the development of case studies, often proprietary in nature. These cases hold considerable value to them because they are internally relevant and provide an outside perspective on their own issues. This facilitates better corporate training exercises and helps senior management learn from past experiences. Organisations also benefit from these studies as it captures internal institutional knowledge and experiences and helps to improve the organisational learning of these enterprises. For the sponsoring firm, there may be a great benefit in creating a common language and culture in the firm. If the case is used widely outside of the organisation, it can also help to inform prospective job candidates and vendors about the firm's values and practices.

Why Case Studies?

For faculty that are trying to build their own case writing centres or just trying to develop their own collection of cases, we provide below some of the key reasons why we have found cases useful as a pedagogical tool. As the rationale for the uses of cases has been written upon extensively, we will not delve into this at much length here. However, there are undoubtedly very clear benefits to both students and faculty who use cases in their classroom.

A common cry of complaint often heard from students around the world is that the course material is outdated or irrelevant. This can be quite easily countered by developing cases that are set in an environment where the students are based, plan to work or regularly frequent. Teaching exercises that have a great contextual familiarity make it easier for students to relate to the decision that the protagonist has to make and understand the importance and relevance of the concepts the case is communicating. Indeed a case is the ultimate example of a concept. Teachers have always known that using examples is a key technique to motivate learning and enhance the utility of the material.

Additionally, case studies are a means to apply conceptual ideas, theoretical constructs and abstract models to practical, real-world business scenarios. Cases place students in real-life situations, forcing them to identify with the protagonist and to think on their feet and come up with practical solutions to a plausible problem.

When a case study is being discussed in the classroom, students are engaged — they are not given a chance to sit back. They are forced to come up with viable options and decisions, which requires problem solving skills and often, out-of-the-box thinking. The use of cases in the classroom turns students into active learners rather than passive receivers, helping them develop critical thinking and decision-making skills. It also ensures that the students are indeed involved in the class, as opposed to the instructor-centric lecture that may or may not be received well by the students.

Case discussions naturally enhance dialogue and debate and encourage participation in the classroom, which enhances the interpersonal skills of students or corporate trainees. A comment or recommendation by a peer needs to be heard, introspected upon, and possibly opposed by a counter argument. Using cases, students learn to collaborate and improve their communication skills. Watching and listening to others' solutions can be one of the most eye opening experiences for students. They often learn new ways to think, as others are able to organise and solve quicker, more effectively, or better than they do. Alternatively, watching others struggle or miscomprehend seemingly simple concepts helps students to be better communicators as they realise the spread of competencies.

For the faculty, the classroom experience changes when teaching with cases. It becomes a far more interactive session, and enables the teaching process to move up a natural progression curve from lecturing to facilitating (which is where the case studies come in), and on to coaching.

Having written their own case, the faculty is intimately familiar with the company and the case study. They 'own' the case and the learning material that goes with it, which increases their knowledge and self-confidence in teaching the case. Moreover, the classroom participants usually hold the faculty member in greater esteem. They consider the faculty member to be a case expert and might feel free to ask more questions.

Developing case studies also helps the faculty build and maintain contact with the practitioner world. Finally, developing industry- or institution-specific material can also contribute to the faculty's research.

Besides academia, cases have a wider appeal/advantage for practitioner communities for a variety of reasons, such as enhancing one's consulting practice, or being used as training tools in organisations.

A Case and a 'Great' Case

The difference between writing a case and a 'great' case can be explained using the acronym: S-T-O-R-E-Y! The goal of a great case is ensuring that it includes the following:

Summary

Allows for a solid summary of insights and learnings. This is typically the introduction of the case.

Theories

Enables the instructor to teach the theories or concepts of the day. This would be the teaching objectives for which the case is being written.

*O*rients

A good case should set up for future learnings, and/or offer opportunities to tie to past concepts.

*R*elevant: to the students (and the faculty!)

The case provides students a peek into the challenges and decisions made in the 'real world'. It must, therefore, be relevant to what the faculty plans to teach in that session.

*E*ngages

The case should be such that it keeps the student's attention from wandering. It should be a good, exciting and engaging story.

*Y*ields

And finally, reading the case and the ensuing case discussion should offer insights into practice, and provide an opportunity for the students to see how challenges should or should not be handled.

Each of these elements will be covered in later sections of the book.

The Two Cardinal Questions

There are two key points we reiterate ever so frequently in all our case writing workshops — what we refer to as the two most critical questions to keep in mind while starting to write a case. The first is, "What do you plan to teach through the case?" and the second, "Who is your audience?"

The Teaching Objective: "Before you start, know what you want to teach."

Ultimately, cases are about education, about bringing the real world into the classroom. We shall discuss more on this point in the next chapter, where we argue for the cases that should and should *not* be written. But in brief, a good story which does not have a clear teaching objective is NOT a good case!

"Begin with the end in mind" is one of 'The 7 Habits of Highly Effective People', mentioned in Stephen Covey's bestseller — this advice also holds true for the case you intend to write! You should know what you intend to teach even before you begin to write the opening sentence of your case study. In fact, developing teaching goals is the starting point for every case study, and choosing the organisation as a setting is a vehicle for the concept(s) you want to teach. The teaching objective should not be an afterthought, or an idea that comes later, but instead must be the thread that runs through the entire case study.

Focusing on the teaching objectives helps to organise your thoughts about the company and convey the facts and vignettes that are essential to stimulating the readers' learning journey. This will also help you avoid the pitfall of writing a meandering story with many exciting details but ultimately an ineffective teaching case. Media is replete with interesting business stories that inevitably catch our attention. While some could be a great lead for developing a teaching case, it is advisable to vet each story through the lens of teaching objectives.

Knowing the Audience: "Who are they? What is it they are looking for?"

The second question — knowing your audience — is about pegging your case at the right level of complexity. The difficulty of a case study lies in the complexity of analysis required to reach the outcomes and answers, the number of concepts that are discussed therein, and its presentation (i.e. to what extent the discussion points and answers are "given away" as hints in the case study). For instance, if the case is complex and dense, the likelihood is that it will not work in a classroom of inexperienced undergraduates.

Similarly, writing a 'simple' case for a group of executives would not be a wise idea — the discussion would be uninspiring and a lacklustre one at best, and would be over in no time! More subtly, you may want to understand what type of undergraduates or executives you are writing for. A case written for the first term course may need to be simple as the students have little formal training in the area. Similarly, junior executives and senior executives have tremendously different roles in a company and the types of problems and information that they can process may be different. We will reiterate the importance of these two factors in upcoming chapters.

Plotting the Case Study Journey

The remainder of this book has been divided into four sections.

The first section, comprising Chapters 2 and 3, is essentially the 'reflective' part. It details how you plan a case, search for a relevant story, find a lead, and reach out to the company/decision makers.

The second section, comprising Chapters 4 and 5, focuses on the case design, preparing a case proposal that details the case synopsis and teaching objectives, and writing the case draft, keeping in mind some common conventions.

The third section, comprising Chapters 6 and 7, is largely focused on some of the writing and administrative activities that will help you refine your cases. This section addresses the editing process, getting approval from the company, testing the case study in the class room, preparing the teaching note, and determining possible publication avenues.

The fourth and final section, comprises Chapter 8. It provides some concluding tips for writing an exceptional case and teaching notes.

SECTION 1: Searching for a Story, Planning the Type of Case to be Written, Finding a Lead, Developing a Case Proposal, and Reaching Out to the Company/ Decision Makers

Chapter 2

SOURCING THE CASE AND DEFINING THE TYPES OF CASES

Where do cases come from? On the one hand, cases are everywhere and can be sourced from diverse and varied avenues. Good cases, however, are few and far apart. The most common mistake (and we use the word 'mistake' knowingly) of the novice case writer/instructor is to write any story that comes their way. A good article in the newspaper, a student or an executive eager to explain the company's strategy, a description of an exotic company in a new territory or market — everything appears to have potential. This is probably one of the biggest potential pitfalls of case writing, as these great stories may not make for great cases. This chapter will discuss how to source a case, and also describe some common types of cases.

Sourcing the Case

Let's look at different scenarios.

The cases you don't want to write or shouldn't write

Good stories often fall squarely in this category! These may be sourced from companies or senior executives with whom you have a relationship, and they would like you to write about them. There is an outside chance that you end up with an interesting business issue, challenge or dilemma. However, if you are not so lucky, that case could become a mere PR story that is vaguely illustrative of the organisation and its challenges. In writing such cases, you often run the gauntlet of internal stakeholders that wish to embellish or sanitise the case for public consumption. Indeed, such stories often need to be run by legal, communications and other senior executives, as each of these departments wish to place their firm in the best light. These stories often get hijacked as writing journeys (a.k.a. fluff pieces) rather than an effort in writing a factual teaching tool. Most importantly, such cases are difficult to teach. Unfortunately, such cases most often come your way, and the offer to write the story is often very hard to refuse.

The next category — the cases you should not write — while seemingly easy to define, is the hardest to abide by. Cases often start out as great stories, except that they are just that — a story. As a faculty member or case writer, you need to ask yourself, "Is this really a case?" You can certainly tell the story in class or even share a newspaper clipping, but this does not make it a case study. Remember that cases must generate class discussion, and have something in them that will allow intelligent people to disagree, primarily because the outcome is not clear cut or the decision-maker could have taken a number of equally plausible routes to reach the outcome.

The other kind of cases that you need to think about before commencing are those where the events you plan to write about are dated. Cases should, by and large, be current, i.e. the events should have occurred in the last three to five years. In today's fast-paced business world, cases often lose their relevance beyond this time frame. However, there are some 'classic' cases that have been taught for decades in the classroom. On the whole it is better to consider writing about a more current topic, especially when the case has a significant technological or historical orientation.

Finally, howsoever exciting the story line may be, ensure that you have access to accurate and reliable information (data, timeline, quotes, etc.) about the situation you plan to write about because it can be extremely difficult to get hold of informed sources.

The cases you should write

Now let's assume the company is a well-known one and they have done something quite exceptional or gone through a situation that provides discussion material and/or problems or solutions which fit perfectly within your curriculum. However, you have no access to the company. Should that stop you? Not really. One way is to reach out and contact a person related to that company. Especially for large companies, we have found that if we try hard enough, there is invariably someone we can reach out to who can put in a good word on our behalf.

At a university, you could consider reaching out to leading firms through colleagues enrolled in Executive Education and Executive MBA courses, or those associated with the Alumni Office and other centres. Similarly, an organisation could look for contacts among its partner network, both as well as external. One word of caution though (which will be discussed later at some length) — do ensure that the contact person in the company (the case lead or the pro-tagonist) is sufficiently senior as you would subsequently need the case to the reviewed and approved by the organisation. Junior employees may not be able to secure approval from, or even access to, some of the senior layers and departments of the organisation.

For smaller firms that could potentially be a good source for a case (entrepreurship and scaling-up are two teaching objectives that come to the mind), do try to contact the founder or chief executive.

If you have a great idea but limited access, rest assured, some of the best cases have been written from publicly available sources, what we call 'secondary data' cases. These will be discussed in the next section.

Types of Cases

Next, you need to determine what kind of a case you are going to write.

Inquisitive or illustrative

An inquisitive case pushes the participants to arrive at a decision and helps to explain a concept or theory. These cases are very popular with the American business schools. The second category, more popular with the European schools, is a descriptive, qualitative case study that is used to explain or teach a concept more directly. In the European model, the problem, the decision, the reasoning and the results are all given to the students. However, in the American model, the students may need to first determine the problem, then supply the analytical muscle, and thereafter make the decision. Both styles have their advantages and disadvantages.

Let's take the example of one of the cases we have written at SMU, "The Fukushima Nuclear Disaster: Leadership in Crisis".[3] The synopsis of this case is as follows:

> The case describes the events and conditions surrounding a critical decision that Masao Yoshida, the plant manager of Tokyo Electric Power Company's (TEPCO's) Fukushima Dai-ichi nuclear power plant, must make on March 12, 2011. A day earlier, a massive 9.0 magnitude earthquake hit the region where the power plant was located. This caused significant damage to the

---

[3] Jochen Reb, Havori Joshi & Yoshisuke Iinuma (2012). The Fukushima Nuclear Disaster: Leadership in Crisis. Singapore Management University, Case Study SMU-12-0014.

Fukushima Dai-ichi nuclear power plant, disabling both the regular and backup power supply. Without cooling, the nuclear reactors' temperatures would steadily rise, ultimately leading to a meltdown of the reactor core. Yoshida decides to inject fresh water into the reactors using fire engines — a procedure that has never been tried before. He soon recognises that the limited fresh water supply will run out and so decides to replace it with seawater. Less than twenty minutes after the seawater injection has started, Yoshida receives orders from senior management to stop the injection. What should he do?

This case stops at a point where the participants are pushed to make a decision — should they flood the nuclear reactor with salt water from the sea? From our experience of teaching this case in the classroom, the participants typically ask for more data and more time to make the decision. The instructor explains how the protagonist too did not have that luxury before arriving at a decision. The tension in the class increases, and often new dynamics emerge. For instance, an American student may say, "Yes, he's the guy on the ground. There's no question of it. He should actually flood it with sea water." But a Japanese or Korean student may say, "He should follow the orders of the boss." As in most case discussions of these types, there is rarely a 'right' answer. But it is evident that this kind of a case also enables the live illustration of cross-cultural variances in decision making to come through — one of the key teaching objectives of this case. These types of inquisitive cases enable a great classroom experience full of rich learning.

An illustrative case can work equally well in the classroom. There is a very popular case study written on Nintendo's Wii.[4] Some years back, the video game console market consisted of two dominant players — Sony with the PlayStation and Microsoft with the XBOX.

---

[4] Ali Farhoomand, Havori Joshi & Samuel Tsang (2009). Nintendo's Disruptive Strategy: Implications for the Video Game Industry. The University of Hong Kong, Asia Case Research Centre 09/428.

Both product offerings were getting smarter, more complex and advanced, and also more expensive — and then the Wii was introduced. Small and simple, at a fraction of the price of its competitors' offerings, the Wii had a motion-sensor wireless remote that enabled superior interaction with the players. The Wii took over the game console market by storm. This case had little of the excitement of tension or decision-making on the part of the participants — and yet, it proved to be a bestseller case. Why? Because, it was a wonderful illustration of the concept of disruptive innovation which had then become very popular. It was also a timely, relevant and topical case study for students. Needless to say, it was picked up by faculty around the world.

Hence, both inquisitive and illustrative cases can work well in the classroom, as long as they have a well-defined teaching objective. The key difference is that while the latter reinforces clarity of a concept or theory, the former enhances investigative critical thinking skills.

'Real' or Disguised

There is a definite advantage to writing cases about well-known, 'real' companies. And this is, in a large part, due to the students' ability to relate to them. It is not surprising that most students would be far more enthused to discuss a case on Coca Cola's entry strategy in Myanmar, rather than an anonymous CC drink entering an anonymous ABC country.

However, one may also write and publish disguised cases. This often happens when the protagonist or the company does not give permission for their name to be used. For example, we had written a strategy case study on a jewellery company in South Korea, and just when it was sent for a case release, there was a huge crisis in the family and the company was headed for liquidation. We were asked to disguise the case to such an extent, that it became almost fictional — not only were the numbers changed and the images deleted, but we also changed it from a jewellery business to fine watches and pens. We disguised all the names and even changed the country of business from South Korea to Japan!

We have also written disguised cases where the story line is fictional, but the numbers are real. In the case of the Singapore REITs (Real Estate Investment Trusts) case study, data for the three large Singapore property dealers was publicly available (from company websites and annual reports), but the story line of a protagonist at a credit rating agency evaluating the REITs was entirely fictional.

Field cases, Secondary data cases and 'Armchair' cases

Case studies use two key sources of data — primary and secondary. Primary data is proprietary and is collected or observed directly from the original source. Secondary data is based on data that has already been published and is publicly available.

As can be intuitively understood, a case study based on primary data benefits from the richness of insights or from the personal touch of original quotes and personal experiences — aspects that are often missing in cases based on secondary data. Additionally, while collecting primary data, you have the opportunity to probe and dig a bit deeper on subjects or issues. Thus, primary cases, which are more common than secondary data cases, are developed in close cooperation with the company and the protagonist, and typically involve several interviews with different stakeholders within and outside the company.

Interestingly, we have also found that it can be much easier to write cases based on primary data, of course assuming you have a forthcoming set of people to interview! In such instances, the bulk of the case is written based on the interviews. Combined with some basic background information, such a case is normally ready with minimal effort and time.

But to succeed in completing primary cases, you need to be a project manager. This is because interviews need to be scheduled (often with busy senior executives), data has to be sourced, collated and presented, and the case has to also be reviewed and approved by the company/protagonist. And it is the latter — approval by company/protagonist — that can often make the process lengthy and difficult as the case cannot be published without a written case release. In this sense, cases using primary data can take considerably more time to develop. Delays in approval happen quite frequently, and hence it is critical to get sufficiently senior managers involved in the case writing process from the very start, and also deliver the final product in a timely manner before those people change roles, resign, etc. It is also far more difficult to change or update a primary data case, as one has to go back to the company for a new case release — and it's quite likely that your contacts in the company may have moved on. These are the kinds of situations where it may be better to run with secondary data from the very start.

Sensitive topics which carry public scrutiny, legal repercussions or the potential for significant financial or legislative impact are almost always best handled by a secondary data approach. Additionally, when writing cases on corporate governance and ethics, it is preferable to use secondary data instead of interviewing the company as, on sensitive topics, you may not be able to present a completely unbiased view. An honest account will unlikely get company sign off, unless the event is really dated, in which case they may not mind — but your students will!

Where else do secondary data cases work? An example would be a bestseller case we wrote, "Brewing the Perfect Blend: Starbucks Enters India". We found that there was plenty of data and quotes available online, and trying to engage with the company for primary data collection and eventually authorisation would only delay the release of the case unnecessarily. The Nintendo Wii case, mentioned earlier, is another good example. There was enough information available from published sources, including quotes from key company executives, and the event and the teaching objective were both very clear, so there was no reason to delay the process by trying to approach the company.

The last category of cases is what we refer to as 'armchair' cases. These are fictional documents about imaginary companies and/or people, and about events that have not really occurred. They may be loosely based on some authentic data, but would typically lack the complexity or richness of a primary or secondary case. They are usually based on the author's experience, and are used for generating class discussion or introducing basic concepts.

> While all three types of cases can be equally effective in the classroom, our experience has been that it is largely the primary data cases that win awards or gain recognition in case writing competitions.

Chapter 3

PLANNING THE CASE

Once you know the teaching objectives and have decided what type of case (primary data, secondary data, armchair) you will be writing, it is time to develop an outline. Writing a good case study is like putting together a giant jigsaw puzzle — once you have all the pieces of the puzzle, you need to piece it together. As in a puzzle, where one typically starts by putting together the edges of the puzzle to create the outline, in a similar manner, it is good to start writing a case study by first designing the outline!

The Case Proposal

Outlining is an essential step in organising the process

Given that the case study is quite meaningless without a teaching objective, the case proposal *must* also include what would be taught through this case. We have found it very useful to prepare a Case Proposal Form that lists out the following (refer to **Exhibit 1** for a template of the Case Proposal Form):

- Case Synopsis: This is the summary of the case, or the introduction, which is covered in more detail in Chapter 5.
- Conceptual Framework and Learning Objectives: This is the core of the Teaching Note that elaborates the concepts to be taught through the case. More details are provided in Chapter 6.

- Suggested Student Assignments: This section lists out the questions the students will be asked after reading the case. It is a critical piece to think through, as the case must provide enough information and data for the participants to discuss these questions.

A well-prepared and comprehensive case proposal form works as a wonderful outline for both the case and the Teaching Note. Moreover, the proposal form serves as a compass throughout the entire case writing process.

Sourcing the Data

It is hard to complete your case without data

Having prepared the case proposal, the next step is to ascertain what kind of information and data you need to include in the case. Without proper information, the students will not be able to answer the questions you raise, or be able to understand the concepts you wish to teach. This is hence the thinking time!

There are two broad categories of data that are typically required to write a case. The first is what we refer to as the staples, which include information about the organisation, its history (as relevant) its management and financials, etc. Much of this information can typically be found in published sources. And if it is about a small start-up or an individual with no online presence, you will find that the company executives are quite comfortable to share this information. In order to give the case some context, you would also need information about the industry the company operates in, the location/geography, and possibly the context of the business environment, all of which are easily available through public sources.

The second type of information that is essential is specific to the decision being made in the case, the problem, or the opportunity.

Without hesitation, any skilled case writer would tell you that this information is most vital to building a teachable case. Unfortunately, it is not as readily available and it may be more difficult to source. As can be expected, the type of data required would differ across cases, and in large parts, depends on what you want to teach.

Even if one has access to primary data, it is always wise to do secondary research first and collate whatever is available in the public domain. This background research will help you in three ways. First, it gives you a better grounding and background on the company and its industry or environment. This third party information is often less biased than the account the company management will provide you. Or, at least it offers an alternative perspective. Second, your breadth of understanding of the organisation and its industry will help you to ask more thought-ful and probing questions, which will help you develop a case that is truly insightful and differentiated. And third, having an idea of what information is available, what can be obtained, and what can't be found, helps you to organise your company inter-views. Knowing what you absolutely *must* learn from the primary process is an excellent starting point in organising your inter-views. Another point to be highlighted here is that as you collect secondary data, be sure to reference it as you go along. Otherwise, you may end up revisiting all those sites just to get the correct citations.

Motivating the company to share data: the easiest cases to complete are those that have willing sponsors

Understandably, busy company executives, who will likely be the case protagonists or part of the interviews, have to be sold on the idea of writing a case study. We have found that most are quite happy to share information that will be used for academic pur-poses. Often, they believe this is their way of giving back to the society. They may also want to build a relationship with the university and its students as it could be useful for recruitment or training purposes. Agreeing to participate in a case study also serves as a good way for companies and their executives to get exposure and awareness about their firm, particularly in markets where they may not have a strong presence. Industry councils and associations may also interested in case studies to know about best practices or exemplars.

Oftentimes, the protagonists are eager to observe and participate in the classroom discussion when their case is being taught, to get insights from the faculty and the students about the corporate challenges they face. They also like the fact that the case can be used to enhance their own internal knowledge repository. And finally, it is a good ego boost for the protagonists to see their name appear in published case material!

Once you have the in-principle approval from the company, it is time to get ready for the interview.

Getting the interview right

The initial contact with the company will most probably be via email or an informal meeting. Following this is the scheduling of the interview, when you will get an opportunity to ask questions about the business event, decision or dilemma. As mentioned above, prior to the interview, it is a good idea to gather information about the company and the industry from secondary sources, as well as some information on the contact person.

For the interview, you should be prepared and ready with the following information:

- Explain what case writing means: It is not every day that the management has a case written about the organisation.

The interviewees often have questions about their role in writing the case and how they will/can help you. Focus on the pedagogical purpose of the case and the fact that it is not an investigative/critical piece. Explain your role and the other people that will be involved in the process: Who will be the contact person, the faculty, the case writer, etc.

- Assure confidentiality: This is very important. State categorically that the company/protagonist has the last say on the case, and if they do not agree with something in it, they can request for it to be changed. Also mention that the case cannot be published without a written case release from them. If insisted upon, you may want to sign a non-disclosure agreement with the company, although we would recommend you have this first reviewed by your legal department to ensure that you are not taking on an undue onus and liability.

- Explain the case writing process: Most of all, the company/interviewee will want to know what is involved in the process — that is, what is expected of them and how much time they are expected to contribute to the development of the case. We have found that planning for a one-hour interview with each key contact person is usually sufficient, and this may be shared with the company as a realistic ballpark figure. In addition, the company/protagonist will typically review one or two drafts of the case before signing the release.

- Access to the 'right' level: Do try and understand the organisational hierarchy, and identify the key contact persons in the company that you would like to meet and/or interview. As mentioned earlier, we would strongly recommend that you try and get access to the very top/senior management, otherwise you can run into problems at the sign-off stage — the middle level managers may be happy to share their experiences and discuss the issue at stake, but they often don't have the authority to approve the case. Unfortunately in these instances, when the individuals with the sign-off authority receives the case for approval, they are hesitant to sign off as they were not kept in the loop and don't have the full context of the case writing process or mission. Oftentimes, the fact that their inputs have not been taken, and they have not been quoted in the case, can become a hindrance in obtaining the release.

- Question list: You may also wish to send in your questions or request for materials in advance, so that the interviewee can be prepared for the topics.
- Audio recording: You need to take permission to record the interview so that you are able to capture authentic information and the protagonist is not misrepresented in any way. If you wish to have a video recording, this is a good time to mention that too.
- Closure: Close the email/meeting with a formal request obtaining permission to write the case.

One important point to remember is that you must try and get multiple sources of information within the company. A single source can often be mistaken or biased, and that could be quite embarrassing for you when data is refuted or contradicted by others.

To conclude, if information for the case will be obtained through an interview, set the tone upfront by preparing accordingly. Do not overstay, and before you leave, try and set a date for the next meeting. Also mention that you will send a detailed plan and draft interview questions before the next meeting. Finally, if the meeting has gone off well, ask them to share whatever material they can before the next meeting so that you are better prepared and take up less time of the interviewees.

Data Collection from the Interviews

Once the interviews are scheduled, do remember to adhere to what you have mentioned above in terms of the time commitment of the interviewees.

Most of all, we would recommend that you keep an open mind during the conversations. Often, you have gone into the meeting with a particular topic in mind, but in the course of your conversation you realise there is another issue which could be equally or more fascinating. Share your teaching objectives with the interviewees and ask if they have any ideas that could be interesting for the students to discuss and learn from. Think if this can be weaved into your case, or be written up as a Part B of the same case, or as a separate case altogether! (Note: you may also move such topics to the Teaching Note or the epilogue. Such material, while not featured in the case, may be useful background for instructors that want to feel comfortable with the company and competent in discussing the company facts, information, performance and operating principles.)

Once you return from the interview, do transcribe your recording or clean up your notes as soon as you can. This is really helpful as the longer you procrastinate, the more difficult is it to recollect all the nuances and emotions that you experienced, which could add robustness to your case. So it is best to start writing the case study within a day or so of completing the interviews.

SECTION 2: Writing the Case Study, Keeping in Mind Some Common Conventions

Chapter 4

DESIGNING THE CASE

Case writing has a truly unique style. You want a case to be interesting and catchy with a little spice thrown in, and yet it is not a piece of pure fiction. It is also not a purely academic or research piece, where the style is probably a little less important than the content being conveyed. A case is somewhere in between, and what you have to do is ensure that all the writing skills you have learned over the years — both in creative writing as well as more formal outlets — are put to effective use as a case writer. While having a flair for writing is undoubtedly a great skill and advantage for a case writer, what really helps is knowing the science of case writing, which consists of the structure and the common conventions followed while writing a case study.

Organising the Data

Once you know the concept(s) you want to teach, have decided what business story would work as a good example to illustrate that concept, and have collected most of the data that needs to go in the case study, it is time to start writing the case. So, where does one start? We identify below the key 'ingredients' that have to be whisked together and moulded into making the perfect case study.

You have to think about how you want to organise and present the data you have. So spread it all out — just like the many pieces of a puzzle — and identify the thread that will run through the entire case and bind the story together.

Start organising the data in a way that brings out tension and drama in the case story. The starting point is the question or the key challenge that you wish the student to answer. You may decide not to make it absolutely clear in the case and leave it to the reader to decide (this holds true for particularly complex cases), but as a case writer, this is the key to your success — as this is the dilemma/challenge/question that you wish to craft the case around. The Case Proposal Form should greatly help to formulate the case outline. (Note: If you find yourself editing cases or teaching new case writers how to get started, you will want to spend time getting them to think through the proposal and determine what is the dilemma, challenge or question.)

Then think of the cast or the key players. Identify the protagonist, who is the person whose role you wish the student to take on. You may want to focus on the following questions: Who are the supporting characters? Do we need quotes from all of them? Are there opposing views to add some friction?

Then think of the scenes or the key events that have played a significant part in leading up to the key question. It is important to have the timeline right. Typically cases are written in chronological order of the events as they have occurred.

Then there are the props, or the surrounding macro-environment, which impact the decision. You have to determine much of this — what should constitute the main body of the case, and what should appear as exhibits illustrated at the end of the case study.

Designing the Case Study

Finding the right format for your case

Perhaps the question most on top of mind for a new case writer would be about the format of the case. There is no one-style-fits-all format that one can follow when writing a case study. The format will depend on the type of case and the type of information you have collected. We have experimented with a variety of structures — a negotiation case, for instance, could be a conversation between two parties. A case can even be just one page long, which provides the key data and very little else in terms of context. And then there is the realm of multimedia or simulation cases, which open up entirely new formats of developing cases.

But do think upfront whether the teaching purpose will be met by a single case, or a multi-part one. If it's a multi-part case, and you plan to distribute the second part, Part B, and subsequent parts in the classroom, then you need to keep their length short so that the students get time to read it during the session without taking up too much of the 'teaching' time. There are many advantages of a multi-part case. First, it generates good discussions at different stages of the event or situation and allows the tension and story to unfold gradually. While the background data can be presented only once, each subsequent part can deal with a different issue. And you can add different players and scenes more elegantly, rather than throwing them all into the script of a single case! It is sort of like a weekly detective show. The A, B, C, etc. cases are like different episodes of the show. The detective (in this case, the student readers) has a single crime to solve each week. A series of cases can be written based on the same storyline, if useful to another course teaching objective. This allows for integrative potential.

The Case Title

A good title can help educators find you

A good title to the case study goes a long way in attracting others to read and use it. On case distribution platforms like Harvard Business Publishing and The Case Centre, the number of cases available in every discipline runs into several thousands. It is hence very likely that faculty or trainers searching to use a published case may not even look at yours if the title does not sound interesting! The title needs to be self-explanatory, include key words and the name of the company, and be catchy. It should succinctly answer the following: What is the main topic of your case study? What do you want to talk about?

For instance, the Starbucks case was on a multinational firm's entry into an emerging market, India. So you want to make sure that your title has the words 'Starbucks Enters India'. The full title read, 'Brewing the Perfect Blend: Starbucks Enters India'. Why 'brewing the perfect blend'? Because 'brewing' draws on its association with the coffee industry. And the 'blend' goes beyond coffee to refer to the fact that this entry was done in partnership with a local firm, and not by Starbucks alone. It also referred to 'blending' or adapting to local market conditions. Of course, we may be expecting too much from our readers to catch all the subtleties of the title, but one has to try! What is really important, and must be clearly stated, is that this is a case about Starbucks entering India — the rest of it is really just making it attractive enough to catch the reader's attention.

The Inverted Pyramid

A classical approach to writing

The case format that will be discussed here is perhaps the most traditional one, and has been used in the majority of cases written by most business schools. It is a common writing style used by news agencies too, referred to as the 'Inverted Pyramid' format. In essence, the Inverted Pyramid is a structure in which the key data is provided upfront at the beginning of the case. This section, termed the '*Introduction*', acts as a summary of the case, and enables the participant to quickly gain most of the relevant and critical information, along with the discussion questions, without reading the full case.

The Introduction is followed by the *Body* of the case, which starts broadly, first providing the background of the industry, then of the company, and moves on to specific areas and/or events, ultimately leading to the question, decision or dilemma. In other words, you start on a broader note (talk about the macro-environment, the industry, etc.), then get a little more specific and talk about the company, then within the company you may want to talk about a particular department, then within that department you may want to talk about the actual problem. You may then discuss the issues at hand. So you become more focused, leading up to the decision to be made, and/or a "next what?" The case would typically end with a conclusion that raises the questions to be answered and which you have probably already listed in the Case Proposal. The body of the case needs clear headings and the text must be divided for clarity.

Last of all, there are the *Exhibits*, which may be financial statements, tables, figures, maps, and pictures. Do note that figures and tables can be very important in providing a great deal of information in a concise, readable and common format — the way students will probably get future information in their profession or career.

We would suggest that the starting point to drafting your case study would be to first put together the Introduction, an outline of the Body of the case (that is, the headings and subheadings) along a timeline, and a list of potential Exhibits. Each of these components is discussed in more detail in the following chapter.

Chapter 5

DEVELOPING THE COMPONENTS OF THE CASE: INTRODUCTION, BODY AND EXHIBITS

To begin with, every case should include a standard footnote on the first page that may read as follows: *This case was written by Professor XXX and XXX at the XXX University. The case was prepared solely to provide material for class discussion. The authors do not intend to illustrate either effective or ineffective handling of a managerial situation. The authors may have disguised certain names and other identifying information to protect confidentiality.* Along with this disclaimer, you should also include in the footnote the version (date published) of the case, and the name of the copyright holder.

The Significance of the Introduction

The introduction is the taster or sampler to the case. In a couple of paragraphs, it should provide a good lens of the case — telling the reader what the problem is and whose role they are assuming. Treat the introduction as the start of a thriller movie or a drama! It is the catchy first paragraph that draws the reader's attention. It should provide a teaser of the story that is about to unfold, and the event(s) that has happened, and the decision that has to be taken based on the event that has taken place, which is 'what makes the plot thicken'. Experienced case writers will agree that getting the introduction right is like winning a good 70% of the case writing battle!

The introduction should draw the reader in by being relevant, and carrying the right amount of tension to keep it interesting. The reader should be able to identify with the protagonist as soon as he/she reads the introduction. While it should contain all the relevant key information, the introduction should be kept short, not exceeding 500 words. It can start with a quote — oftentimes from the protagonist — which could capture the essence or tension of the case and also highlight that this individual is a key decision player in the case. The quote can also be from a famous personality or book, hinting to what the Teaching Note is all about.

As would be suggested in most training sessions for writing a report — be it for journalism, research, or even a police investigation — any good introduction or summary should answer the 5Ws: Who, What, Where, When and Why. Answering these questions would typically suffice to get the storyline right.

(i) Who was involved?

Who is the protagonist, and whose role should the reader assume? One key point to keep in mind is to avoid what is termed as 'protagonist confusion' — having two or more equally strong candidates for the protagonists role mentioned upfront, as that could confuse the reader. There are only a few exceptions to choosing the primary protagonist, for instance, where the case is, say, one of a two-party negotiation.

A common question asked is whether it is essential to have an individual protagonist, or can it be omitted? Or what if the protagonist is a group, like say, the Board of Directors? While there is no sure-shot formula for writing the perfect case, do recollect that one of our key objectives of case writing is to put the students in the shoes of the decision-maker. And your case analysis will take on a very different hue depending on whom you have identified as the key decision-maker. For example, if you want to write a strategy case for a company, it may not make sense to have the Sales Manager as the decision-maker. The protagonist should ideally be the company's CEO, or a Board member, or the Head of Strategy. Alternatively, the protagonist could be a front-line employee facing a normal experience that they might routinely encounter. In summary, the protagonist should reflect the level at which the information to answer the case would be presented.

(ii) What happened?

This is the key mission behind writing the case: What is the nature of the problem the reader should discuss? Or then, if it's a qualitative case, what is the theory or best-practice principle that you want to teach the student? The answer to this question should have already been elucidated in your Case Proposal, and is also the first cardinal rule to writing a case. Be careful not to give the plot away at this stage — what you really want to do is excite the readers and motivate them sufficiently to read the rest of the case!

(iii) Where did it take place?

The location where the case is set is important not only to provide context, but also to measure how much data needs to be provided to the students. Intuitively, one would need to give more background material on say, Laos or Myanmar as compared to China or the United States. However, we would recommend keeping the second cardinal rule at the back of your mind at this point, and think of your audience. When you publish the case, you really do not know in which part of the world your readers will be located.

In a case workshop we taught in 2014 at a small university in Asia, only two of the 25 participants had heard of McDonalds! Hence providing some background on the location is always beneficial. Professor Philip Zerrillo, author of *The Case for Cases: Teaching with Cases*, would often say:

> *You have to think about who may be reading your case. If a kid in Iowa is reading your case set in the streets of Mumbai, you have to give him or her a sense of the environment that the case is taking place in. They should be able to feel like they can hear the streets, smell the food, and see the colours. Part of what we provide in a case is an opportunity to transport the student from the classroom to far away and mystical places. The case can not only be a vehicle for teaching a theory, but for opening the eyes of its readers to a whole new world. This is when theories become robust and minds become flexible.*

(iv) When did it take place?

Providing the temporal coverage and getting the timeline right in a case study is necessary for ensuring its flow and lucidity. The timeline is also important as there is typically a trigger to the case — an event that is a cause for concern (in an inquisitive case) or a significant milestone has been achieved/not achieved (in an illustrative case). The trigger is also usually the point at which the case ends, called the cut-off point.

There are different points at which you can cut the case. For instance, it could be when the decision/problem has to be identified; or at the investigation/analysis phase, the decision phase, the implementation phase, or evaluation phase. A classic example of this could be a mergers & acquisition case study. Depending on when the case is cut-off, the students could spend their time doing a first-cut valuation or due diligence exercise, or how the integration between the two companies should be handled, or even discussing why the merger/acquisition was unsuccessful.

Cutting off the case at different points could result in very different case studies — and would depend on what theory, framework or practice you wish to teach. So the timeline is a crucial component of designing the case study, which should be dictated by the teaching objective and illustrated clearly in the introduction.

Besides the teaching objective, there are a couple of other considerations that you may want to think about when deciding the cut-off point. Is it an interesting decision point? Does it lend itself to some drama and tension? Is the sense of urgency creeping in? If we go back to the Fukushima case (refer to Chapter 2), we note that by cutting it off when the decision *had* to be made, rather than say, three years later, brought in a lot more tension.

You want to make sure that you know the cut-off point as you begin writing, as this is a key organising element to your writing. The point to be kept in mind is that one cannot provide any other data in the case after the cut-off point (after all, you want the students to have only that much information that was available with the decision-maker in reality). This understanding of what information can and can't be included helps you greatly in organising your information and assessing what appears in the case study.

(v) Why did the issue take place?

Why the issue is taking place or why it is important is not only a key part of building the story line, but also essential for the students to know in order to analyse the problem and come up with reasonable alternatives. As such, the introduction should typically provide a brief overview of the company and protagonist, and give a brief run-up to the event that made the particular situation arise, and then go on to outline the same — that is, the issues or dilemmas that need to be addressed in the case, without going into actual specifics.

To conclude, if you answer the five questions explained above, you are assured of a strong and clear introduction. This should serve as a good foundation and put you in good stead for the rest of the case.

Writing exercise

Assess the following introduction, and think what you would have done differently to improve it:

Late in March 2018, on a warm morning, James Tan, the CEO of Royal company arrived in his office, excited to meet with Charles Lim, the Founder and President. Things were falling in place. The local Singapore newspaper had last week covered Royal, and iden-tified the company as a key player in the $800 million television channel business. Its viewership now exceeded all its competitors, and Tan knew that now was the right time for the company to expand internationally.

Assessment of the above introduction in terms of the 5Ws:

(i) *Who was involved? The readers may not be sure whose role they should assume — Tan or Lim. So there is a danger of 'pro-tagonist confusion' here.*
(ii) *What happened? The nature of the problem the participants should discuss is unclear. This could be a case study for teach-ing international marketing and diversification, or also one on persuasive communication skills!*

(iii) *Where did it take place? It is evident from the cue of 'the local Singapore newspaper' that this case is set in Singapore.*

(iv) *When did it take place? In March 2018.*

(v) *Why did the issue take place? There is no clarity or data on the key issue to be addressed in the case.*

This introduction would have to be reworked to provide far more clarity on the decision to be made, as well as some context for making such a decision.

We have provided the example of the introduction of one of our award-winning cases, 'BPI Globe BanKO: Reshaping the Philippines Rural Banking System'[5] in Exhibit 2, which illustrates how an effective introduction can be written using the five questions as a base.

The Body

While the introduction allows for some flair and creativity on the part of the case writer, the body of the case is typically more straightforward; it usually closely follows the Inverted Pyramid structure outlined in Chapter 4, or the format you may have decided in the Case Proposal. For a novice case writer, we would suggest presenting the information in chronological order; this is typically the simplest way to ensure that the story and timeline is clear and easily understood, and also minimises the risk of repeating facts. Frankly, if you are trying to provide the reader with clarity and enhance their understanding, recognise that humans are temporal processors and jumping back and forth in time forces them to pay attention more to the dating of the material than its content.

---

[5] Peter Williamson & Havovi Joshi (2016). BPI Globe BanKO: Reshaping the Philippines Rural Banking System, Singapore Management University Case Study SMU-16-0010.

The first draft of the case study is more of a data dump — adding all the information and quotes in chronological order. It is best to err on the side of adding more information rather than less at this stage, which subsequently can be edited and sharpened. Having said that, do keep in mind that writing at length about the company or the protagonist's background may not be as relevant or interesting as talking about the issue at hand and possible alternatives. This is tougher to source, and most often requires the support of the interviewees.

What follows, not necessarily in order, is a list of tips that can help in writing the case body.

Structure

The first tip to keep in mind when writing the body of the case is that it must be easy to read. Technical jargon or complex terminology should be used only to the point that it is necessary, and if so, should be explained in simple words (ideally in a footnote). The case must also be well-structured. In fact, when we run a case writing workshop, after the participants complete writing the introduction and are ready to embark on the body of the case, we first ask them to write down all the headings and sub-headings of their case on a page and confirm that the structure works. Exhibit 3 illustrates the Introduction and Structure of one of our cases, 'Tata Salt: What to do when a Flanker Brand grows up?'[6] This is a classic example of following the Inverted Pyramid method with clear headings and sub-headings.

Facts versus emotions or opinions

A common error made by new case writers is to allow their own opinions and emotions to reflect in their writing. This must be

---

[6] Philip Zerrillo, Havovi Joshi & SN Venkat (2012). Tata Salt: What to do when a Flanker Brand grows up? Singapore Management University Case Study SMU-12-0012.

avoided at all cost. As a case writer, you have to only present the facts, and leave it to the students to make a decision without clouding their judgment. If you want to add an opinion, it should be referenced to a legitimate and reliable source. These sources include the company (directly through interviews or websites), newspapers, business publications, industry journals, financial analysts, etc. Please note that Wikipedia is not considered to be a reliable source, though it could be a great starting point to getting more information. As an example to clarify the above, you should not state that, "The new product did not have any innovative features". A statement like this should be attributed to either a quote made by someone you spoke to, or properly referenced to published material.

Including quotes

Using quotes is an effective way to break up long stretches of the text, add a human element to the story, and build the tension. Additionally, quotes also serve as an opportune spot to place judgements and opinions. They often provide the students with an opportunity to understand the protagonist's thoughts in their own words, employing their own logic. However, do be judicious about the number of quotes you use — they should not overpower the main text. Allow the urgency of the situation and the emotions of the characters to emerge through quotes, but don't let them overwhelm or sway the reader. Care must be taken to reference the quotes appropriately and respect the confidentiality of the interviews. Be very careful with paraphrasing, and make sure you stay true to the original spirit (this could also prove to be a real roadblock in getting a case released).

Include a conclusion

The case study should end with a concluding section or at least a paragraph. This need not be long, but it should be a quick recap of the situation the protagonist is in, and more importantly, list out the specific questions the reader should consider. These questions may be an elaboration of what is listed in the Introduction to the case. It would also typically include the key questions the instructor will ask in the classroom, and most probably have been listed in the Case Proposal form.

How much data?

Another question that plays on the writer's mind is how much information should be provided in the case? While it is far easier to write a lengthy case that includes every imaginable piece of data, there is also a stronger likelihood that the students will not read it! There is a definite trend towards shorter and crisper cases, and our suggestion would be to follow that as far as possible. Typically, a case study should be between 4,000 to 5,000 words. If there is more background information to be provided, it can be put in the exhibits at the end of the case study.

Only critical information should be mentioned in the body of the case, and that which was available to the protagonist at the time of the decision. In other words, the students should experience the same challenges as the protagonist: shortage of reliable information on which to base decisions, shortage of time in which to make decisions, and uncertainty on how the events and the decision unfold. If there is any confusion, go back to review the Case Proposal, and stick to what is relevant based on the learning objectives and student questions you had listed therein.

It is to be noted that the longer the case is, the less likely students are to read it and read it thoroughly. But also, the longer the case, the more superfluous data it may contain. This greatly lowers the instructors desire to adopt the case. Instructors want cases that allow them to teach a reasonable number of important related topics. Long cases with rambling facts about extraneous areas or concerns can bring the instructor into waters that they may not want to swim in. That is, faculty preparation must be much longer and more detailed and far afield as they could get questions from areas that they don't want or are not able to teach. In summary, the shorter and more focused the case, the easier it is for faculty to pick and use.

Use of images

Photographs, images, maps, financial statements, tables and charts, and long, overly-detailed text such as laws, rules, processes, lists, etc. should be placed as exhibits at the end to avoid breaking the flow of the story for the reader, unless it is a critical part of the case. All images should be referenced appropriately. In particular, it is important to check the copyright of photographs and images taken from the Internet.

Exhibits

Most commonly, exhibits appear after the case body and include financial information; additional background on the company, industry and its key competitors; tables, figures and maps; pictures and images; etc. Do remember that the exhibit must be referred to in the text.

When preparing an exhibit, it is important to be clear about its purpose — how does it add to the case analysis? As mentioned in the previous chapter, reviewing exhibits can help students receive information in a standard template that is used in the industry in which they may be involved in future. Exhibits are also useful and concise instruments for communicating large amounts of information, and they lend themselves to analysis and calculations — which adds to the robustness of a case. While preparing the exhibits, do consider the preferable format. For instance, side-by-side comparisons would help with comparative analysis, while a top-down format might be better for calculations.

Also, it is very important to clear all copyrights. For instance, if you are quoting from a newspaper article and have not been successful in obtaining permission to do so, it is best to keep the quote short and then give a web link to the article. However, do keep in mind that links often break, so it may just happen that your readers are unable to access that information/article after a few years. This is also a challenge in providing a web link to say, a YouTube video, and hence, it may be wiser to host your videos on a proprietary website.

Some Common Writing Conventions

For consistency, we recommend deciding upon and following a writing style guide for all cases from your institution. For instance, you can decide whether you want to follow British English or American English. Similarly, you can follow norms regarding the font size and style and spacing for the text, headings/sub-headings, bullet points, etc., and the footnotes for citations. If your institution does not have such conventions listed out, then you may wish to look at those of the publication outlets you are considering.

There are also some common practices like putting the dates first in a sentence ("In 1995, the firm launched Product X" is preferable to "Product X was launched in 1995") and spelling out numbers from one to ten and using numerals thereafter — but there is considerable discretion left to the author. The three conventions that we would like to focus on, given that they are quite unique to case writing, are given below: writing in the past tense, currency conversions, and citations.

Write in the past tense

One of the key differences between case writing and other writing styles is that cases always happen in the past and have a predetermined cut-off date. The information, time, and the decision the protagonist has to make is dependent on the cut-off date. In writing, say a newspaper article, there is a desire to make it seem immediate, relevant and timely. This is not the primary goal of the case. In other words, writing a case is akin to writing about an event in 2015, while sitting in your chair in 2018. While this may sound strange, the timing of a case study almost always necessitates this kind of writing.

Writing in the past tense can also lead to some awkward, and at times nonsensical, statements. Since the case study is not intended to be read at any particular point in time, it must add an implied date to all things that you write. For example, a quick read of the Encyclopaedia Brittanica about the former U.S.S.R. will highlight the point. The article states, "The Union of Soviet Socialist Republics was by area the world's largest country. It was also one of the most diverse, with more than 100 distinct nationalities living within its borders."[7] While this makes good sense when reading it today as the Soviet Union no longer exists, it would perhaps jar the reader to read these words in the past tense in say 1985! But this is for a country — so as you can imagine, organisations tend to change and morph even more rapidly.

Writing in the past tense also brings about consistency as the reader does not keep switching between tenses. However, if it's sounding really strange, remember that quotes can always be written in the present tense. An example would be, "Paul Tan, the CEO said, 'we are happy with the current state of progress'." In a similar vein, one should avoid the use of words such as 'now', 'presently', 'currently', 'today', 'tomorrow', etc. (keep it to the quotes if necessary) — as you want the case to be timeless.

---

[7] Martin McCauley, Richard E. Pipes, Robert Conquest & John C. Dewdney (2018). Soviet Union, Historical State, Eurasia, https://www.britannica.com/place/Soviet-Union.

Currency Conversion

As the world becomes a more global place and some hard currencies rule global finance, most readers are able to relate to the handful of common currencies. We recommend using a well-known currency through your case study, as it may not be obvious to a reader how the currency translates into their own, or for that matter, how much it was worth at the time the case was set. This makes a point of conversion an important point, and more specifically a reference point for the reader. The common practice for cases has been to convert everything to U.S. dollars, so that the reader can understand the local currency quoted with little additional effort.

Citations

A case study is an academic tool, and you want to show the readers that you have used the highest levels of academic integrity in writing the piece. Thus, it is a good practice to cite any piece of information, no matter how small, that you have obtained from another source.

Adding citations as you go along writing the case study is like cleaning up your cooking supplies as you cook; make sure you do it well, or it's going to be a lot of hard work at the very end! Each time you visit a website and take even a sentence from it, make a reference immediately — otherwise you will have to visit them all over again when you start referring at the end.

Decide on a style of referencing and be consistent with that throughout the case. Some of the common citation styles are the Chicago style, Harvard style or APA. We prefer using footnotes for citations, but if there are too many of them and its distracting from the main text, you may wish to use endnotes.

SECTION 3: Preparing the Teaching Note, Getting Approval from the Company, the Editing Process, and Possible Publication Avenues

Chapter 6

PREPARING THE TEACHING NOTE

The Teaching Note is a guide to how a case should be taught by faculty. It describes the questions to be asked, the possible answers to those questions, and the key concepts and theoretical constructs to be taught through the case. Additionally, it would include suggestions on the time to be spent discussing the case, the structure of the discussion, and perhaps how the whiteboards in the classroom might be used. While cases without Teaching Notes are available through several distribution platforms, this is really not recommended and ideally you should not publish a case without the Teaching Note.

In essence, a Teaching Note should be treated as a conversation between two faculty members in which one is trying to discern whether or not they should use the case written by the other, and how they are going to teach it. As you put the Teaching Note together, you need to recognise that there is a convention by which instructors evaluate the information about the case. But, they are also looking for clues, tips and resources for teaching the case.

As the Teaching Note provides an in-depth analysis of the case, it also demonstrates how conceptual models can be applied in order to solve or understand the underlying issues presented in the case study. This enables lessons from the case study to be consistently gleaned in any classroom. Do recollect that the teaching objectives were the starting point of your case, and the questions you plan to ask the students would have driven the writing of the case.

The first draft of the Teaching Note has already appeared in the Case Proposal, albeit in a succinct form. In a sense, the Teaching Note has always been there in an outline form, guiding the case author as the case study is being drafted.

While it can be expected that a long case will have a lengthy Teaching Note as it has more points to discuss, in fact, the opposite can hold true. A brief case does not provide much background or context to the reader, and so the Teaching Note becomes lengthy as it provides more detail of what can be taught with that case study. For example, one of our most popular case studies, 'Memaksa Steel',[8] is a one-page case study, but the Teaching Note runs into 14 pages! This is because there is a lot of analysis and number crunching that can be done with this case. Additionally, information often leads to restrictions on the direction the case actors can take. In short cases there are fewer management restrictions, hence the discussion can be multi-directional.

Components of a Teaching Note

To begin with, as with the case study, a Teaching Note comes with a standard disclaimer on the covering page that reads as follows: *"This Teaching Note was written by Professor XXX and XXX at the XXX University. This Teaching Note is designed to be used with case: 18-0XXX. The case was prepared solely to provide material for class discussion. The authors do not intend to illustrate either effective or ineffective handling of a managerial situation. The authors may have disguised certain names and other identifying information to protect confidentiality."* Along with the above, do include the

---

[8] Philip Zerrillo (2012). Memaksa Steel, Singapore Management University case study, SMU-11-0001.

version (date published) of the case, and the name of the copyright holder.

An outline of a good Teaching Note is as follows:

- Executive summary
- Case issues or learning objectives
- Suggested lesson plan for a typical session
- Student assignment questions
- Suggested teaching plan (assignment questions with the answers)
- Additional follow-up questions (optional)
- Wrap-up
- Epilogue (optional)
- Suggested readings

Each of these components is discussed in detail below.

Executive summary

This is the case synopsis, which should present a succinct and clear description of the case. It should convey the main issues of the case in about 500 words. To a large extent, the executive summary can be copied and modified from the Introduction of the case study.

Case issues

The Teaching Note should state the learning objectives for the case, which should also be brief and concise to allow a first time reader to assess whether the case relates to, and is relevant for, their course. There should be a minimum of three separate learning objectives presented here. This should also explain how this case is relevant to the course teaching objectives and the audience. You would have likely already prepared this when drafting the Case Proposal.

There should be a sentence or two that states the level of case difficulty, and which audience it is suitable for, i.e., undergraduates, postgraduates, executives, or all of them.

Suggested lesson plan

This section provides a guideline to teaching the case. It explains the recommended steps through which the case can be taught, and also proposes the time to be spent on each section. It should also suggest whether the case should be handed out prior to, or during, the class. An example of a suggested lesson plan would be as follows:

Activity	Instructional Strategy	Duration (min)
Discussion about the case (company background, change management, position of the protagonist in the company, etc.)	Class Discussion	10
Discussion about challenges faced by the protagonist	Class Discussion	20
Group discussion about particular challenges	Break Out Group	20
Wrap up of Case (discuss strategies discussed, key learnings and epilogue)	Lecture	15

Student assignment questions

The questions, too, should have already been listed in the Case Proposal, although they may have been modified as the case progressed. These should include all the key concepts and teaching objectives that the instructor plans to cover in the classroom through the case. It typically begins with an opening question, or an ice-breaker, that may recap some of the important facts of the case study, such as: "What is the main focus of the case? What happened? Why is that important?" Thereafter, it would proceed to questions like: "Why could X be called a good leader?" that could be used as a vehicle to elaborate say, the principles of good leadership.

Suggested teaching plan

This teaching plan provides the answers to the Student Assignment Questions. One very important point to note while writing the Teaching Note is *not* to merely repeat what is already mentioned in the case study. This is the space for the author to detail the concepts or principles on which the case analysis is based, and to provide insights into the answers of the questions and the possible alternative solutions that readers might offer. So, if for instance, the question is on the competitive strategy that the company used to enter China, the answer should not just parrot what was mentioned in the case, but instead discuss it in terms of the concepts to be taught, e.g. Porter's Five Forces, the BCG Matrix, etc., as the note should offer insights into how the case facts could be organised, analysed and distilled into useful arguments to support or refute a potential strategic option.

The case analysis can also be structured along the concepts listed in the learning objectives, whereby the first section head would be say, "Understanding the Concept of Disruptive Innovation". Then the first question could be a discussion on innovation in general, followed specifically by disruptive innovation, what the company has done that makes it a 'disruptive innovator', how other players in the industry are reacting to this situation, etc.

Additional follow-up questions

While writing the Teaching Note, it is important to be clear about the teaching objectives you had in mind — but do keep in mind that a case may be used by other faculty to teach a different topic — particularly if it's a complex case with many underlying layers. It is also possible that you might consider using the same case to teach a different topic for another course or at another time. For instance, one of our SMU case studies, 'Zara in China and India'[9], can be used to teach students about competitive advantage, retailing, and the development of unique business models in the fast fashion industry; as well as the challenges that a firm from the developed world faces when it expands into emerging markets. So the 'Additional Follow-up Questions' help you to go beyond your own immediate teaching requirements and provide a more robust set of questions that would further class discussion outside of student assignments, or provide additional teaching material for faculty who teach the case for another purpose. This is an optional section of the Teaching Note and should be used as and when required. If you are an instructor and have used the case to teach different topics, it is appropriate and useful to share the different order of questions, emphasis of topics and analysis in different teaching situations. Again, the Teaching Note is a conversation among instructors to help them teach to their best.

Wrap-up

The wrap-up section simply ties together and reiterates the learning objectives and course concepts that are to be taught through the case study. It can be quite brief, ranging from two to five sentences. While it may be short, the wrap-up is an essential element in using a case. Instructors need to think about how to summarise

---

[9] Nirmalya Kumar, Sheetal Mittal & Havovi Joshi (2018). Zara in China & India, Singapore Management University Case Study, SMU-18-0003.

the point of having this case in their class. For cases that are used in standardised core classes or very broadly-taught topics, the wrap-up can be a bit longer as it easier to tie it to other course concepts or past and future learnings.

Epilogue

This is the question the students really want answered: What finally happened to the company or protagonist? What is the status today? This is also the section we recommend that the author continue updating in the Teaching Note, over time. It is an optional section of the Teaching Note and should be used as and when required. But just be aware that instructors, like the students, are curious how the story ends.

Suggested readings and resources

This lists out readings that are recommended for the instructor to peruse before teaching the case. It might also point them to videos, instructional aids or analytic tools that can help them to teach the case better. Today, we are seeing that more and more Teaching Notes have audio or video supporting materials.

Some Additional Tips

The Teaching Note should follow the same guidelines used for writing a case study in terms of being concise, clear and comprehensive. It should also follow the same writing style (font, bullet points, citations format, etc.) as the case. Unlike the case study, however, the Teaching Note is always written in the present tense.

And finally, prior to publication, it really helps to test the case out in the classroom. This is also the 'acid test' for ensuring that your case and teaching note are complete and fulfil your teaching goals in the classroom! It also allows you to better relay helpful insights and tips into how a case might be interpreted by the students that have experienced it — helping your fellow instructors to better use your case.

Chapter 7

GETTING READY FOR PUBLICATION

The Editing Process

The case and Teaching Note have to be edited for clarity, comprehensiveness and conciseness. The editor also has to ensure that the two documents are well-aligned — so the questions provided in the Teaching Note can be answered by the data provided in the case study, and that the Teaching Note actually explains how this can be done.

At SMU, our cases and Teaching Notes go through two separate types of editing. The first is for English language — structure, grammar, punctuation and typos — the kind of issues that creep in even with the best writers. The second set of edits comes from a faculty review board.

To elaborate, following several rounds of internal reviews, when the case authors are satisfied that the case and Teaching Note are complete and read well, they would request the two documents to be submitted for editorial review, where a professional education consultant and copyeditor will evaluate both, based on their teaching merit as well as quality of writing, and suggest possible edits.

The next version of the case is then submitted for peer review, to a member of a ten-person faculty review board based at SMU and other universities around the world. One person from the faculty review board, who is specialised in the subject, topic or domain, will review the case and Teaching Notes based on its teaching merit and provide feedback on how the case can be further improved.

If the case is based on field research, i.e. it is a primary data case, it will, at this point, be submitted to the company for review. Once the company (and the case authors) agree on a version of the case, the company signs a Case Release form (discussed in the next section). If substantial changes are made to the case following this point, then a new release will have to be signed prior to publication.

Classroom testing is conducted to better refine the case for classroom use. The case may then be revised again, and finally submitted for final edits and proofreading.

Case Release

A primary data case cannot be published without a signed approval from the organisation/protagonist. This is a template that should be approved by your institute. In brief, the Case Release should state that the individual (in his own name or as the representative of the organisation) has read the case and approves the disclosure of all the information contained therein; and the use of the case by the author/institute for their academic, research and teaching activities, as well as publications.

Ensuring Academic Integrity

Prior to publication, the case and teaching note should be uploaded into an anti-plagiarism software to ensure that academic integrity has been maintained. This would cross-reference the text to provide a final quality control check on references and citations.

Typically, the university that is publishing the case study retains all copyrights, unless the case study is being jointly developed with another organisation (in which instance the copyrights are shared), or if a proprietary case study is being developed for a client on a fee basis (in which case the copyrights belong to the client).

Publication Avenues

There are several channels through which you can publish your case and gain wider visibility. These include the Case Centre, Harvard Business Publishing, Ivey Publishing, Sage Publications, etc. These institutions and publishers provide clear guidelines on their website on the process to get accepted for publication.

Another route to publishing would be to keep an eye open for case competitions. For instance, Emerald Publishing and the European Foundation for Management Development (EFMD) conduct case competitions and the winning cases get published on their distribution channels.

SECTION 4: Concluding Tips on Writing a Great Case and Teaching Note

Chapter 8

WHAT ARE THE INGREDIENTS
OF A GREAT CASE?

After having written over 200 cases and presented at numerous case writing workshops, we put together a list of what we believe to be the seven most important factors that contribute to making a great case.

Make Sure It's Not Just a Good Story

A good story makes for a newspaper article, it is journalism. *You have to make sure that the case teaches something which is relevant* for the classroom. It's not an opinion. It's not a piece of research. It's not a solution. It's a pedagogical tool. It must always include a managerial issue that makes participants analyse the issue by taking on the role of the protagonist. The case must teach a relevant and important issue, at least for the audience it is taught to. It should be a sufficiently interesting issue that has consequences the students can relate to. This is where the two key cardinal points mentioned in Chapter 1 are reiterated yet again. The best case is one that works for your class — it is pitched at the right level and supports what you want to teach that day.

The Case Should Pose Questions that Require Decision Making

The case should ask the students a question, the answer to which is based in either theory or knowledge of best practice. For instance, if the case asks, "Should the CEO be fired?" — the student's answers should include not only an analysis of the firm's appraisal and lay-off policies, but also perhaps a larger discussion on what are the traits of a strong leader. Students not only have to break down the case into smaller sections to understand what is really happening, but thereafter they also have to put it all together again to present a coherent and defensible set of arguments and recommendations.

A Good Case has an 'Exciting' Story Line

Think of it like a television soap opera that has surprises and controversy thrown in! Imagine the protagonist as the main actor, who is struggling with a problem (managerial dilemma). Some background is provided. Then there is a conflict. He or she doesn't get what they want. Options are considered, either alone or in consultation with other players. New ideas emerge! And the story plays on... And all this must be covered in a 21 minutes episode, or in your case, in 8 to 10 pages! There should be sufficient opportunity for students to debate.

A Good Case is Well Written

A good case is well-edited, is grammatically correct, and easy to read. The case has a personal touch with quotes from executives in the company or the protagonist, and describes formal and informal processes and the culture of the company. It is well structured, with clear headings and sub-headings. Finally, it should also contain contrasts and comparisons which make it memorable for the students, and easy for them to relate to where, say, the firms fits in the industry. Comparing the company to big players and the small ones helps add context to the case.

A Good Case Provides 'Current Useful Generalisations'

There are some limitations to using case studies. These include the case being a snapshot of a situation, or one that uses unique events to illustrate concepts, but the event itself may never repeat. As an example, we hope that there is never another Fukushima nuclear situation — but even so, the key learnings from the case (dealing with leadership in a crisis), are relevant, useful and replicable.

A Good Case Should be the Right Length

While the number of pages is a key consideration (and remember, it is far easier to write a longer piece than a shorter one), what we refer to here is that the case should have the right amount of data — not too much, not too little. It should give what is needed to make defensible arguments on behalf of the protagonist. While it is recognised that students can go online to search for additional data or the 'answer' to the case, it is preferable if the case can stand on its own. In fact, this also makes it possible for faculty and firms to use the case for closed-book examination purposes.

Be Adventurous!

While you master writing a case, do also step out and look at including supplemental teaching material like excel spreadsheets, videos, etc. with your case study. Today there is a shift in the class-room from the written word to multimedia, and cases are also following a similar route.

Conclusion

For decades, case studies have been a cornerstone of the pedagogy employed by leading business schools to prepare their students to step into the real world of business, face challenges, and make decisions. A case study is not expected to provide solutions, in fact there may often be no 'right' answer — it just lays out the facts and gives sufficient data points to the students to arrive at defensible arguments. It is hence a powerful learning tool an instructor can employ to facilitate discussion, analysis and critical thinking.

As you get started, you will find that your ability to write better and better cases will come naturally with practice. After writing a few cases, you will be able to better organise your teaching plan, think through the teaching points, prepare for your interviews and ask the right questions. As you develop these competencies, the nuts and bolts of writing the case will get easier and you will flourish. So, be bold, get started and have some fun with writing cases!

Exhibit 1

CASE PROPOSAL FORM

Faculty Name: _____

Co-author (s): _____

Date: _____

Proposed Case Title: _____

_____

Functional Area: _____

Industry: _____

Source: ☐ Published material (secondary data)

☐ Field research (primary data)

Case Synopsis:

This is the summary of the case

Learning Objectives:

Please provide a brief summary of what you expect students to learn from the case. For example: understanding and managing cultural differences; convergence of digital and traditional media; the impact of innovation on industry dynamics; understanding the conflicts between marketing and operations in an organisation when making planning decisions.

Suggested Student Assignments:

Please include examples of the types of questions students will be expected to respond to or the type of analysis you expect them to perform.

Examples:

What role does corporate culture play in this case?

How might Company X have avoided this negative publicity?

Exhibit 2

AN EXAMPLE OF THE INTRODUCTION TO A CASE: HIGHLIGHTING THE 5 W'S

BPI Globe Banko: Reshaping the Philippines Rural Banking System[10]

The excitement in the room was palpable. It was early November, and John Rubio, president and chief executive officer, BPI Globe BanKO ("BanKO") had just announced that BanKO had doubled its cumulative customer base from January to October 2014 to reach 966,000 customers — putting it well on track to achieve its stated mission of building a business by 'banking the unbanked' in the Philippines.

Established in 2009, BanKO was the Philippine's first mobile phone-based, microfinance-focused savings bank. At that time, statistics showed that eight out of ten Filipinos did not have access to a bank. A few informal moneylenders provided some 40% of small-scale business lending in the market, at interest rates that could touch around 240% per annum. The population living in 40% of the Philippines' municipalities did not have easy access to a physical

---

[10] Peter Williamson & Havovi Joshi (2016). BPI Globe BanKO: Reshaping the Philippines Rural Banking System, Singapore Management University, Case Study SMU-16-0010.

73

bank branch. Less than 10% of Filipinos had a credit card. BanKO intended to address these issues by leveraging its combined assets in banking and telecommunications through a partnership between the Bank of the Philippines Island (BPI), the oldest operating bank in Southeast Asia; Globe Telecom, a leading telecommunications company; and the Ayala Corporation, one of the largest conglomerates in the Philippines.

BanKO aimed to provide the delivery of a range of banking services through mobile solutions supported by a network of partner outlets. These outlets were existing establishments in the community, such as pawnshops and grocery retailers, which had been selected, trained and accredited to conduct customer identification for new account applications, and perform cash-in and cash-out transactions. They were the critical link to bringing financial services to communities located even in remote locations, ensuring widespread reach and accessibility across the country. BanKO also offered loans to microfinance institutions, including rural banks and cooperatives, and had successfully reached over 400,000 micro-entrepreneurs in the Philippines through these partner institutions.

While BanKO's performance, particularly over the past year, had been encouraging, Rubio realised that the team had yet to firmly establish that BanKO's platform and business model was indeed viable and sustainable over the long-term. In addition, he would need to work out how the business could be further expanded, while ensuring that the ecosystem did not become too unwieldy to manage.

Exhibit 3

AN EXAMPLE OF THE CASE OUTLINE

Tata Salt: What to do when a Flanker Brand Grows Up? (A)[11]

It was the beginning of 2011, and Parag Gadre, the assistant vice president of marketing and strategy at Tata Chemicals Limited ("TCL"), was deep in thought. He had just reviewed the latest data from his marketing unit, and noted that the "I-Shakti" brand of salt was continuing to grow and perform exceedingly well. In the five years since it had been launched, it had become the second biggest salt brand in the country after the flagship brand — Tata Salt from Tata Chemicals.[12] Gadre realised that he faced an unusual dilemma, and the time had come to make some hard decisions about I-Shakti. The product, I-Shakti was first conceived as a place holder brand to satisfy the demand that the unit's original flagship product, Tata Salt, could not satisfy, but I-Shakti had now become a 'real' brand that could potentially evolve to be a serious threat to Tata Salt, the market leader.

---

[11] Philip Zerrillo, Havovi Joshi & SN Venkat (2012). Tata Salt: What to do when a Flanker Brand grows up? Singapore Management University case study SMU-12-0012.

[12] According to Nielsen Retail Audit, August 2009, I-Shakti had 14% of the total market share in the branded salts category. For further details, see Tata Chemicals website, http://www.tata.com.

I-Shakti[13] had been launched in 2006 as a refined iodised salt targeted at the lower end, regional markets. The brand was intended to be an intermediary between the bulk salt sold in many grocery stores, local brands and the branded packaged salt. Unlike Tata Salt, it was not manufactured in-house, but sourced from third party manufacturers, and then packaged and marketed under the I-Shakti brand name. In contrast, Tata Salt was a well-established and comparatively high value added (vacuum evaporated) product, aimed at meeting the needs of the educated consumer in the cities. While the customer segments, markets, attributes and pricing for the two brands were envisaged to be quite distinct, I-Shakti's exceptional success was now beginning to pose a distinct challenge to Tata Salt. Further, one of the principal factors that had motivated TCL to launch I-Shakti was the production capacity constraint at the Tata Salt factory — an issue which would soon be mitigated as the capacity expansion project at the plant was well on track to be completed by January 2012.[14]

Gadre was wondering as to what would be his best option. Should I-Shakti be left to continue growing in the salt market, and perhaps compete directly with Tata Salt? Or should the I-Shakti brand de-emphasise salt, and move out into other product categories?

Salt in India

Historical Significance

The Salt Industry in India

The Key Players in India's Iodised Branded Salt Market

Tata Chemicals Limited (overall company)

---

[13] "I" stood for Iodine, and "Shakti" represented power.

[14] The new capacity for producing vacuum evaporated salt would increase production through put by 33% to 0.8 million tonnes per annum.

Tata Chemicals — the Flavour of Salt (about Tata Salt)

Tata Salt and I-Shakti — the Branding of Commodities

Logistics

Sales and Marketing

The Tata Salts Portfolio — What Next?

Tata Salt & I-Shakti — the Dilemma

Exhibits

Exhibit 1: The Production of Salt

Exhibit 2: The Salt Producing Regions of India

Exhibit 3: India's Salt Market — the Demand-Supply Scenario

Exhibit 4: India's Salt Market — Segment Wise Volume Trend 2008–2010

Exhibit 5: The Logistics of Tata Salt — Factory to the Consumer

Exhibit 6: The Logistics of I-shakti Salt — Factory to the Consumer

Exhibit 7: Cities in India with a Million Plus Population

Exhibit 8: The Tata Salts Distribution Network

Printed in the United States
By Bookmasters